BIRTH OF A NATION
THE ROCKS • SYDNEY

Panographs® by Ken Duncan

FOREWORD

Located in the heart of dynamic and cosmopolitan Sydney, The Rocks is Australia's birthplace. Since The First Fleet arrived in Sydney Cove to settle the area in 1788, The Rocks has been a village with a variety of history, culture and life.

The graceful terraces and tastefully converted warehouses belie the fact that over many years The Rocks was allowed to fall into decay with slum conditions, disease and gangs of thugs menacing the area, until the construction of the Harbour Bridge (1923-1932).

Although this helped to restore some sense of order to The Rocks, by the 1970s there was a public outcry for the area to be restored and brought back to life for the people of Sydney to enjoy. With the future of The Rocks uncertain, The Sydney Cove Redevelopment Authority was established to undertake a massive project of regeneration and restoration.

Today, The Rocks bears little resemblance to the craggy outcrop that was first destined for settlement by convicts and their military minders. The area is now a unique and colourful centre with a bustling village atmosphere where visitors and locals alike enjoy its stunning harbourside setting. Beautifully preserved buildings, streets and monuments are complimented by galleries featuring the work of both well known and new Australian artists, and many of The Rocks numerous restaurants spill out onto the streets for alfresco eating. In addition to Sydney's widest array of speciality shops, the famous Rocks Market displays the city's finest arts and crafts. Set under a sail-like canopy stretching down George Street, dancing, music and street theatre bring The Markets alive every weekend of the year.

In *Birth of a Nation,* Ken Duncan's extraordinary photographs capture the essence of The Rocks and present some of the most striking images of an area that is for many people, not only Sydney's first place, but their favourite place.

The Sydney Cove Authority is proud to be associated with this book.

Bob Mitchell

SYDNEY COVE
AUTHORITY

George Street, The Rocks.

3

THANK YOU

I would like to offer my sincere thanks to the sponsors who have endorsed this project. It is only through their support and assistance that we have been able to produce this book.

Clocktower Square – has become the favourite place to shop in The Rocks. With 21 specialty shops filled with quality Australian merchandise, this popular shopping centre features weekend attractions and exhibitions every month. Telephone: 02 241 1077.

Purescript Reprographics – is Sydney's foremost pre-press establishment and offers a huge range of services including high resolution scanning, colour separations, multi-media and CD production. Telephone: 02 212 3022.

The Old Sydney Parkroyal – the premier hotel location in the heart of The Rocks. Telephone: 02 252 0524.

Fuji/Hanimex – there is no better film than Fuji to capture the colours of Australia. Telephone: 02 938 0400.

Compaq Computer Australia – is the world's largest supplier of personal computers. Telephone: 1800 225 286.

Vision Graphics – the kings of colour film processing in Sydney. Telephone: 02 929 8658.

Page 1 - The Bounty on Sydney Harbour.
Susannah Place, Gloucester Street.

5

Ken Duncan Gallery, 73 George Street, The Rocks. Open 7 days – admission free. Telephone: 02 241 3460

INTRODUCTION

To me The Rocks is the birthplace of this nation. Here the first association between two cultures had a profound effect on a country in embryonic form.

The Sydney Cove Authority is to be congratulated for its responsible and sincere approach to The Rocks. They have preserved the heritage of the area while creating a healthy and balanced path into the 21st century.

The hope of this nation lies in our people – now of many cultures – moving in unity and not allowing division. We are one nation and if we begin to learn from one another, we can look forward to a bright future. For God does not look at skin colour, but at the depth of the heart and its ability to love.

On 26 January 1788 Captain Arthur Phillip raised the British flag, declaring Sydney Cove the farthest outpost of the British Empire. Only a few days later, on 3 February, Reverend Richard Johnson held this country's first church service under a great tree on George Street North. Of this memorable service Marine Lieutenant Clark wrote in his diary "I will keep the table as long as I live, for it is the first table that ever the Lord's supper was taken from in this country".

The tree has gone but hopefully now our Gallery at George Street North will be a sanctuary and provide a constant banquet to the spirit of every visitor, as it displays the wondrous beauty of God's creation.

This book is dedicated to the most important people in my life… God, my beautiful wife Pamela and daughter Jessica.

Ken Duncan.

The Hero of Waterloo hotel, St Patrick's Day.
The Rocks constabulary.

Ken Done reflecting on The Rocks says "It's got this wonderful human scale about it…a sense of real commitment and involvement in the past and, yet, you're in this incredible position where you're right in the middle of the two great icons of Australia – the Opera House and the Harbour Bridge – and surrounded by very modern, very sophisticated, very cosmopolitan society."

Having run his gallery and retail outlet in The Rocks since 1980 – nearly an Australian icon himself – artist Ken Done professes an affection for the area that dates back to his childhood and he fondly remembers the sights while on ferry rides from Cremorne. He expresses gratitude to everybody who battled to save The Rocks when there was talk of wholesale redevelopment.

"I'm glad there were people who had the foresight to understand the need to preserve what, I think, is one of the most interesting locations in Australia. The very first drawings of mine that anybody saw were of Sydney Harbour, the Harbour Bridge, The Rocks and the Opera House. It's an area that's always made me want to celebrate living in Sydney and being an Australian. I don't think I would have done the things I've achieved without that inspiration."

Artist Ken Done in his converted studio.

$\mathcal{E}$very weekend in The Rocks, a sail-like canopy transforms historic George Street – just under the Harbour Bridge – into Australia's most innovative and original street market.

Underneath the all-weather canopy, The Rocks Market reveals a treasure trove of unique, unusual and different products, many that can't be found anywhere else in Sydney. Over 140 stalls display antiques, locally-made crafts, collectables, jewellery, homewares and furnishings. Visitors are also entertained by street theatre, music, dancers and mime, or they can enjoy a break in one of the many cafes and restaurants which surround the Market.

Nestled between 200-year-old buildings and located beside the stunning scenery of Sydney Harbour, no other street market can offer quite so much atmosphere, variety and colour. And come rain, hail or shine, The Rocks Market is open every weekend of the year.

The Rocks Market.

15

The Rocks Market – a fun place to be.

The Rocks Market, which extends into Playfair Street, offers an array of unique gift ideas.

The Bubble Man, performing at The Rocks Market, entertains audiences by floating huge
and colourful soap bubbles high above the crowd.

Every weekend, the streets are filled with colour and activity. Performers entertain with various musical styles
from rock to classical and Latin to jazz as they are here in The Rocks Square.

As guardian to the heritage and history of The Rocks, The Sydney Cove Authority has undertaken a number of archaeological digs in an attempt to unearth the remains of buildings and artefacts that may be of particular significance to an overall understanding of the area's development. Investigating the architecture and artefacts of the past gives Australians important insights into their architectural, social and military history.

In mid 1995, one such opportunity was seized to uncover the hidden secrets of Dawes Point Park. Situated at the north end of George Street underneath the towering pylons of the Harbour Bridge, this area is steeped in the rich history of Australia's first settlers. It was once the site of the colony's first observatory, military battery and a significant Francis Greenway building, but during the construction of the bridge, all this history was thought to have been destroyed or buried.

Archaeologists slowly dusted away the dirt to reveal the hidden history of our past. Enthusiasm at the site was infectious, spurred on by the constant possibility of a new discovery and the uncertainty of the artefacts that further excavation would reveal.

Across tumultuous seas and through fierce unforgiving winds sailors made their way to Sydney. The eight month journey from England, with limited rations but unlimited hazards, must have resulted in many smiling faces as they finally set foot on Sydney soil. The new arrivals were the only source of news from abroad and a tenuous link between homeland and colony.

The sailors' relief at arriving safely was celebrated enthusiastically at the many public houses of the day. The sounds of their carousing echoed through the narrow cobbled streets of The Rocks.

Once trade was established, the merchant navy ships and their crew added a colourful element to The Rocks. They brought with them a vast array of exotic products including seal skins, sugar packed in big bamboo baskets and salt from Cape Verde, all of which were unloaded into the stores lining the waterfront.

The warm glow of the numerous fascinating maritime treasures displayed here in the Bottom of the Harbour Antiques shop reflect and bring to life the spirit of the sea but belie the building's macabre history as a Coroner's Court.

Bottom of the Harbour Antiques shop.
Overleaf - Sydney Harbour.

Trevor Kelly is a colourful local identity who has lived and worked around The Rocks since the late 1960s.
A statue in memory of Trevor's best friend, a cheeky schnauzer dog known as 'Biggles', stands on the corner of Atherden and Playfair Streets.

The Sydney Observatory, on Observatory Hill, was opened in 1858. When the First Fleet arrived at Sydney Cove in 1788,
an astronomer, Lieutenant William Dawes, was among the first arrivals. Dawes Point marks the site of his first makeshift observatory.

The architecture commonly seen around The Rocks often dates back to the early 1800s.

The magnificent stained glass windows of The Garrison Church at Millers Point.

It's perhaps not surprising that artist Charles Billich has chosen The Rocks as the site of his gallery. His early life has many parallels with the struggling formative years of the area while his ardent belief in freedom of thought, multicultural goodwill and a sense of community fit well with today's attitudes and philosophies.

When his birthplace, Croatia, was under the control of communist Yugoslavia, Billich was imprisoned for expressing liberal views and while there he learned the value of tolerance and individual expression. Released after two years, he fled to Austria where he studied art at the Volkschochshule in Salzberg. Arriving in Australia in 1956, he continued his studies at Royal Melbourne Institute of Technology and the National Gallery of Victoria Art School.

"I try to convey spiritual optimism and vitality, visual utopias," he explains, "I want people to be better, to look higher, but as much for their sake as for the sake of the community."

Billich at The Rocks.
Overleaf - The Sydney Opera House from Dawes Point.

The Sydney Harbour Bridge at sunset. A mammoth construction project for the time, the bridge took seven years to complete and was opened on 19 March 1932. For many years it was the largest single-span arch bridge in the world.

Sydney's cityscape at sunset. In recent years, Sydney has blossomed and become a very cosmopolitan city and highly popular destination for tourists from around the world.

A view of the magnificent Sydney Harbour from the roof-top pool of The Old Sydney Parkroyal Hotel.
Overleaf - Sydney Harbour and The Rocks at dawn.

Few Australian hotels boast quite such a colourful history as The Hero of Waterloo which has stood at 81 Lower Fort Street since 1843.

The hotel quickly became a favourite drinking spot for the Garrison troops as well as the local population and, according to legend, it was from here that unsuspecting drunks would be press-ganged into the merchant navy. As the hapless recruit stood groggily at the bar, a trap door would open, unceremoniously depositing him into the cellars below. No doubt dazed and bewildered, he was quickly bundled down a tunnel which led from the hotel to the harbourside and a waiting clipper ready to sail.

Today, The Hero's maze of stone cellars incorporate nothing more sinister than a fascinating museum, but visitors may like to pause for a moment to contemplate a chequered history which also included rum smuggling.

The cellars underneath The Hero of Waterloo hotel.

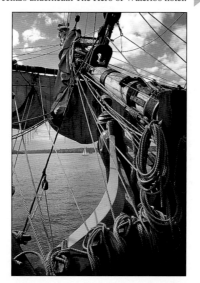

Skilled puppeteers transport audiences to a magical world where strange and wonderful creatures captivate and entertain.

Previous page - The Rocks form the perfect backdrop for the majestic *Bounty*, moored here at Campbells Cove.

The Rocks Puppet Cottage in Kendall Lane offers great family entertainment with regular performances every weekend and school holidays.

Architecture unlocks the tales of our trading past in The Rocks, and here in the Merchants House, its walls, witness to transactions, negotiations and conversations since 1848, could spin many a fine yarn. The only remaining example of Greek Revival architecture in the area, its sturdy presence may not be with us today without the commitment of locals and others like former Builders' Labourers Federation Secretary Jack Mundey who worked tirelessly in the 1960s to conserve the heritage of The Rocks.

The Merchants House and Sergeant Majors Row, George Street.

49

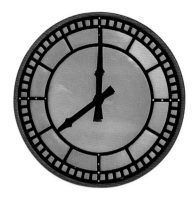

Kitty McMillan, now 81 years old, states emphatically, "I wouldn't live anywhere else. I was born around here, I got married here and I've been living in this house for going on 56 years."

Kitty's brother, Teddy Hartley, moved to Pyrmont after he got married, but has since returned to the place of his childhood and recalls, "In them days, you'd leave your door open and anybody could walk in. My father used to just walk into Tommy Cane's house and sit down and have a feed. Tommy Cane would walk into our house and sit down, he didn't have to be invited."

Kitty remembers, "They used to bring a piano out onto the street and we'd all dance around. There was a few strangers around, but we all got on well together."

Kitty worked in a button factory which stood where the Old Sydney Parkroyal Hotel is today. "Around here years ago, families used to marry into families…so you couldn't talk about anybody because you didn't know if they were related or not."

Inside Kitty McMillan's kitchen. ▶

51

Susannah Place – one of the few remaining examples of a typical 1840s working class terrace,
comprising of four brick houses and incorporating a corner shop.

The interior of Susannah Place. This house was built for Edward and Mary Riley
who emigrated from Ireland in 1830 with their niece, Susannah.

After running shops in some of Sydney's most prestigious suburbs, Dorian Scott recalls visiting The Rocks ten years ago and being so struck by what she saw, she decided "off the cuff" to put in a proposal for a store showcasing Australian designers. Dorian promotes the work of new, young designers whose individualistic creations she feels are symbolic of what makes Australia unique. However, she's equally concerned about the heritage of The Rocks and believes every Australian has a responsibility to protect it for future generations to enjoy.

"I'm a conservationist of this area…it's absolutely unique and very special."

Dorian Scott. ▷

55

Many children visit The Rocks on school excursions and have the opportunity to dress up in convict and Regiment clothes.
These tours are an exciting adventure for young and old and give a great insight into our colonial past.

The passenger liner *Fairstar* docked at Circular Quay – one of many cruise ships which visit Sydney.

Fishing from one of the old piers around the harbour, a stone's throw from The Rocks.

*N*eil loves The Rocks. "Lots of tourists, lots of locals…it's just a great mix," enthuses Neil Perry who is the Owner/Manager and chef extraordinaire at The Rockpool Restaurant. Neil rates The Rocks as "…probably the best place in the whole city to be," and likens the energy levels to those of New York where he lived before.

"I think The Rocks has a very strong personality of its own and people seem to get a buzz from being here. There's a vibrancy down here that seems to be a bit infectious."

Neil both lives and works in The Rocks and matches some of the area's vibrancy and energy in his culinary creations. His idea of a successful restaurant? One which serves, "good lunches and really full dinners".

Neil Perry.

63

A view of Sydney at night, seen across the top of Clocktower Square. The Square is an excellent shopping location at The Rocks.

The Observer Hotel. It was once operated as a public house for sailors during the 19th century and was then known as
The Waterman's Arms (1844). These days it remains a popular place for a drink.

Now something of a tradition, champagne hour starts around six in the evening at Christina's Collectables doll shop in George Street, and she recalls many surprised visitors have suddenly had a glass thrust into their hands. Christina first set up shop in The Rocks in 1985 and became interested in dolls during the bicentennial year when she was besieged with requests for an Australian doll. Today, she has craftspeople across the country hand-making original designs which delight both locals and visitors alike.

Wilson started helping out a few years ago and now describes the shop as a "very nice headquarters". Christina, who's also lived in The Rocks for the last decade says "it's like being part of a small village community...intimate, friendly and wonderful!".

Christina's Collectables.
Overleaf - View of Sydney from Observatory Hill.

The southern side of the Harbour Bridge looking toward Luna Park.
Mural painting on the side of the Harbour Bridge.

79